Maggie's Story:
A True Story of Love and Courage

by
Lois M. Werfel

Cork Hill Press
Carmel

Cork Hill Press
597 Industrial Drive, Suite 110
Carmel, IN 46032-4207
1-866-688-BOOK
www.corkhillpress.com

Trade Paperback Edition: 1-59408-352-5

Library of Congress Card Catalog Number: 2005933622

1 3 5 7 9 10 8 6 4 2

DEDICATION

To Maggie, my faithful companion and dear friend, who taught me many of life's lessons.

To Frederick D. Piper V.M.D. and his dedicated staff, whose skill and compassion brought Maggie and me through many rough times.

To the Central Pennsylvania Humane Society, for without them Maggie would never have entered my heart.

To my family and friends who shared my love for Maggie.

SPECIAL THANKS

To Kathy Peterson for proof-reading.
                        And
To Judith A. Bertram for proof-reading and final typing.

TABLE OF CONTENTS

Maggie

Chapter 1
The Adoption

My story began on a lazy winter day. It was March 31, 1989 to be exact. The Humane Society was about to close for the day when in walked two ladies.

Being quite inquisitive I wiggled free of my littermates and hurried to the front of the cage. This was my big chance. If I played my cards right by acting cute, lonely, and lovable, I just might get picked this time.

"Meow! Meow! Here I am! Look at me," I demanded.
"I'm adorable."

I reached my tiny paw through the wire at the front of the cage and touched someone.

"Yippee! I've been noticed."

One of the ladies stopped right in front of me. She stooped down to pet me through the wire cage and I really put on a remarkable show for such a little kitten.

"I did it. I surely did it this time," I said to myself.

My little heart was thumping loudly with excitement.

Then the lady stood up and walked away and my heart sank to the bottom of my four little paws.

As the lady moved on her friend stood like a sentry next to my cage.

The lady I had touched moved ever so slowly as she peered into each and every cage along the wall.

Then she stopped.

"Oh no," I screamed.

She's interested in that prissy, longhaired, orange and white cat with the biggest fluffiest tail I had ever seen in all my six weeks of existence.

The assistant at the shelter spoke to the lady for a minute or two before handing her a small cardboard box. She opened the door of the cage and gently placed the orange and white kitten into the box.

"It's over! It's all over," I cried.
I walked slowly back to my littermates.

Then to my surprise the lady and the assistant headed straight for my cage. As the door opened I ran toward them as fast as my little legs would go.

"Please," I pleaded.
"Take me!"

For a moment or two I could hardly breathe.

Then the lady lovingly picked me up and gently kissed the top of my head.

She smiled warmly and said, "This spunky one is definitely a keeper."

I was in love in an instant.

"Hurry! Put me in the box," I shouted.

She put me in the box and handed the assistant some green stuff. Then she proudly signed some papers that made me hers.

It was 5:45 in the afternoon when we walked out into the cold March air.

I never looked back.

Maggie and Molly

Chapter 2
A Name All My Own

Yeow! What's that?"

In the excitement of the moment I had forgotten the lady had put me in the box with the longhaired orange and white, the cat with the long whiskers and the big fluffy tail.

I was emotionally exhausted from all the yelling I had done so I wiggled into the corner with my new furry friend.

The two ladies giggled and talked. I wasn't sure what they were saying but the one who had signed the papers that made me hers, tenderly covered both of us with her sweater to keep us warm. I closed my eyes and went to sleep.

In no time at all we were being carried into another strange place. I felt warm and lazy. Then two pair of hands lifted the orange and white and me out of the box and set us down in our new home.

"Wow, this place is a palace," I thought to myself.

Maggie and Molly

At first I was somewhat apprehensive. One room alone was one hundred times bigger than my cage at the shelter. After a nod and a kind word from the lady I scampered about looking over my new surroundings. The orange and white was somewhat timid but she too moved about with wonder in her eyes.

After a short time the lady took us to another room to show us something special. It was a pretty blue box with fresh smelling clay litter inside.

I was first to figure it out, so I showed off and used it. I clung onto the side and somersaulted into the box. Then I scratched and scratched to cover it up. Litter went flying in all directions. The orange and white took her turn and the lady said,

"Good kitties, you are very smart for such little ones."

As darkness filled the sky the lady held us on her lap. She kissed each of us and in a rather serious voice said,

"I am a human and you my little friends are felines, better known as cats.

Yep, from day one the lady always told us the truth. We're cats, she's a human.

"That's it," I said. "I will always call the lady my Human."

The orange and white and I played for awhile, wrestling and rolling about on the floor. We frolicked from room to room smelling our new surroundings. Then after a few bites of kitty food I noticed that my Human had disappeared.

I called out, "Human? Human? Where are you?"

Mom and Molly and Maggie

I guess I had started to miss my littermates too. I searched the house frantically. At last I found my Human taking a catnap under a heap of blankets. I nestled snuggly along her neck and that is where I stayed until the next sun.

That morning after breakfast my Human kept muttering to herself. She went through a litany of names. None of which seemed to suit her. Then she stroked the head of the orange and white with the big fluffy tail and the long whiskers and said,

"Molly you are such a pretty girl. I love you."

"Prissy is more like it," I thought.

My Human continued the litany of names. Now my papers said that I was a Calico. For a moment I thought my Human was going to name me Cal.

"Yuk!" I thought. "I'm a girl and I want a girl's name too."

My Human rambled on for a few more minutes until the name Maggie spilled from her lips.

"Maggie! That's a perfect name for you."

She then scratched both my ears to make it official. Once in awhile she'd slip and call me "Love Bug" but I didn't mind at all.

You know once in awhile I'd slip too and call her "Mom". She loved it.

Later that morning, after Molly and I had been named, Mom picked up a strange looking apparatus and started talking to herself. At first I meowed because I thought she was talking to me. I didn't understand.

I knew she was talking about Molly and me. (Later I found out it was called a telephone.)

When she put the funny apparatus down she looked at us and announced that we would go to meet "Grandma" the following weekend.

I remember wondering whether Grandma was a feline or a human just like mine.

Grandma and Maggie and Molly

Chapter 3
To Grandma's House

I had lived in my new home for seven suns now. On the morning of the eighth sun my Human had been hurrying about gathering all sorts of things. She placed them in a neat stack near the front door.

I couldn't quite figure out what my Human was doing. One thing I did know was that she wasn't giving me the usual amount of attention that I deserved or had grown accustomed to.

I have a vivid memory of sticking my pink little nose up in the air and walking away to pout. On my way to the kitchen my patience had worn thin. Grumbling to myself I motioned for the orange and white, with the big fluffy tail, and the long white whiskers to join me.

"Let's go!" I shouted to Molly.

In a flash my tiny body had raced toward the dining room curtains. In one giant leap I was hanging by all fours to the delicate threads of the sheers with Molly just beneath me. There we were stuck fast like two plastic statues.

In unison Molly and I meowed in our loudest voices.

"Help! Help us please!"

Mom heard our desperate pleas and came running and saw what we had gotten ourselves into. Then she stopped dead in her tracks.

"Molly! Maggie! Not my sheers!" She shrieked.

After a firm scolding, Mom freed us from our trappings and gently placed us on the floor. Instead of the usual kiss on the top of our furry little heads, Mom shook her finger back and forth and said,

"Stay off my curtains and sheers. You cannot be naughty and act like this when we go to Grandma's house."

She continued by telling us that we would go up the mountain to spend the weekend with Grandma. We looked at Mom with big sad eyes and we promised to be good the rest of the day. That had been our very first scolding.

I quickly learned that my Human used several funny sayings. As she left for work that morning she turned and said,

"Don't stick beans up your nose, play with matches or call the boys."

Then she promptly left for work.

Molly and I had finished our breakfast and we chatted about our first scolding. Naturally, Molly blamed me for the whole incident. Then she went off to play with a silly toy mouse. I curled up for a little catnap still wondering whether Grandma was a feline or a human like my Mom.

As I recall, Mom got home from work a little earlier than usual that day. She made many trips to the gizmo that she rode in. Back and forth she went until all the things she had piled near the door that morning had been placed inside the gizmo.

On her last trip back into the house she brought a small blue cage for Molly and me to ride in. Being curious creatures we both stepped inside to sniff it out. Then the door closed and Mom set the latch.

"Off we go," she said.

My last memory of being caged had been at the shelter. Molly and I both shook with fear.

"Oh no," I thought. "I should have been a good girl this morning, but I just couldn't help myself."

"Let me out of here!" I protested.

"I'm yours! Please keep me."

"You signed the papers." "Remember?"

Nothing I said seemed to matter. Out the front door and down the steps we went, straight toward the big green gizmo that Mom rode to work.

My Human set us on the front seat next to her. She turned the key and we were off. I cried softly over and over again, but my Human would not relent and set me free. Molly sat huddled in the corner of our prison, shaking like an autumn leaf.

As the riding machine moved along, I discovered that I had a keen sense of direction. A sixth sense told me that we were not moving toward the shelter, but were heading in a new direction. As we made a steady climb around hills and curves I knew that we were going up the mountain to meet Grandma. I was quite relieved. I proudly walked to the back of the cage to comfort the orange and white.

After riding for some time the gizmo came to a stop.

"We're here," Mom announced.

Grandma was standing watch at the front door. She could hardly wait to meet her newest grand-children. She hurried from the house and moved quickly toward the gizmo.

"I'll carry the girls," Grandma said.

She lifted the cage and carried us into her home. At last my question was answered. Grandma was a human just like mine.

She was a jovial old lady with gray hair and a twinkle in her bright blue eyes. She would soon celebrate her eightieth birthday.

"Wow!"

Grandma fell in love with Molly and me. She was such a pushover for treats. All we had to do was meow and Grandma would run for the treat can. Mom said that Grandma was going to spoil us.

"That's a laugh," I thought.
"We were already spoiled before we got here."

Now I was a natural snoop. While Grandma and my Human were playing cards, I went off to investigate. In no time at all I had gotten myself into a pickle. I had climbed onto the hamper in the bathroom and jumped across to the washer and dryer that sat back into a little alcove. As I crawled along the back of the dryer I lost my footing and fell. Since I had already been in trouble that morning I decided not to yell for help. I was scared though.

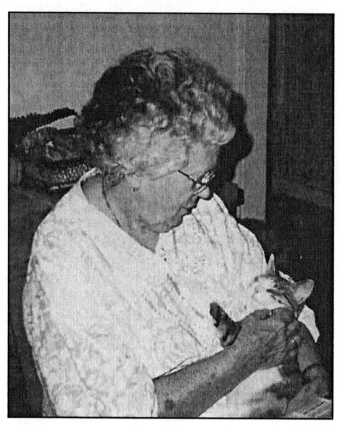

Grandma and Maggie

It seemed like forever until Mom and Grandma stopped playing cards. I had begun to wonder if I'd be stuck behind the dryer for the rest of my life when I heard the shake of the treat can.

"Oh no," I yelled.

I knew that Molly would awaken and beat me to the treats. In a newfound panic I screamed:

"Help! Help me! I've fallen behind the dryer and I can't get out."

Mom searched frantically for me. Then she realized that I was in the bathroom. It was the smallest room in the house, yet she couldn't see me anywhere.

"Oh no," she said.

At that very moment she knew that I was down behind the dryer.

I could hear Grandma laughing in the background. My Human wasn't laughing though. She had a worried sound to her voice.

"I can't reach her," I heard my Mom say.

"What are we going to do?"

I yelled up at them, "Call 911! They'll know how to rescue a little kitty."

Grandma had an apparatus like Mom's and she picked it up and called for help. In no time at all a strong young man had pulled the dryer out and had set me free. I licked his hand and thanked him for rescuing me.

"Now where's my treat?" I asked.

"Oh Maggie, what am I to do with you?" Asked my Human?

The weekend had gone by quickly. It had been the first of many happy weekends, holidays and summer vacations spent with Grandma. She spoiled Molly and me, just like Mom did.

Maggie and Molly

Chapter 4
The Clinic

A few suns after our visit to Grandma's house my Human again drug out the dreaded blue cage. I had to admit that it was nice to look at, but Molly and I hated being on the inside peering out.

"Let's hide," I said to the orange and white.

"Follow me Molly."

Being the wise little kitty that I was, I had scouted out a hiding place for just such an emergency.

We scampered toward the bedroom and I quickly led the way through a small hole in the box spring mattress.

"Mom will never find us up here," I giggled to myself.

Molly sat staring in disbelief as we waited quietly in the dark.

Then we heard the voice that had become becoming so familiar to our ears.

"Molly, Maggie, where are you?"

"Quiet," I whispered to Molly. "Don't make a sound."

"Come on girls," Mom continued. "Today is your first visit with Dr. Piper at the Lakemont Veterinary Clinic and we can't be late."

As we laid in silence we could hear Mom moving about each room of the house searching for us. She looked in the basement, under the sofa, behind the old claw foot bathtub and in every nook and cranny in the house. I felt kind of bad, but not bad enough to give up our secret hiding place.

Finally my Human returned to her bedroom again. I remember holding my breath so that I wouldn't purr. Just as Mom got down on all fours, Molly let out a loud sneeze and gave our hiding place away. Mom laughed when she spotted two little lumps sagging from the box springs.

"You little stinkers," she said as she loosened the corner of the box spring to lift us out.

"I can well imagine whose idea this was," my Human said as she placed us inside the cage.

My mind was racing and my heart was going thump, thump, bump, thump. After all I was just a tiny kitten and I hadn't a clue as to what a clinic might be. Off we went. Molly and I meowing in protest all the way.

In a matter of minutes Mom announced our arrival. Wide-eyed I had quickly surveyed the surroundings while the orange and white, with the big fluffy tail and the long white whiskers, laid hiding at the back of the dreaded blue cage.

Once inside the clinic a lady politely greeted my Human. If I remember correctly Mom called her Miss Receptionist.
"Dr Piper will be with you shortly." She said.
"Tell him to take his time," I mumbled to myself.
While Mom completed some paper work I picked up the scents of other creatures, not all of which were cats like Molly and me. When I looked toward the back of the cage Molly's ears were flat against her head. She looked rather funny. I knew then that she was frightened.

All of a sudden the outside door to the clinic opened and a rather huge dog and a very small lady entered.
"What's he doing here," I asked?

Mom said, "Hush, Love Bug. That's not kind." She picked us up cage and all and set us on her lap while I sat staring that big fellow down.

Molly's curiosity got the best of her; she crept ever so slowly to the front of the cage to take a peek. Then she did a strange but wonderful thing. She licked the side of my face and I kissed her in return. I knew at that moment Molly and I had bonded as sisters even though we were not related. We cuddled closely and chatted about our earlier adventure inside the box spring mattress.

Miss Receptionist returned and took us into a small room. She introduced Mom to Dr. Piper. Mom opened the door of the cage and lifted Molly to a small table.

"It's all right Molly," I whispered.

"This is Molly." My Human said proudly.
"She's the bashful one."

"My, she is a lovely kitten." Said Dr. Piper as he turned her over and checked her from end to end.
"We will start her on her shots today."

I heard a faint little meow as the doctor handed Molly back to Mom. Molly went eagerly back into the cage.

"Oh no, it's my turn." I thought.

Just then Mom scooped me up and handed me to a man in a white coat.

"Maggie meet Dr Piper," said Mom.

I meowed politely then tried to wriggle free.

"Maggie is the ornery one," my Human said laughingly.

Dr. Piper listened to my heart, felt my belly, opened my mouth, checked the inside of my ears and he even lifted my tail. At that point I had become rather indignant and let out a loud hiss that startled both Mom and Dr. Piper.

"Maggie," Mom scolded, "that is not a polite way to act. Dr. Piper was just making sure that you are in good health."

After I had my initial shots and some medicine for Kitty congestion Dr. Piper rubbed the top of my head and gently handed me back to Mom.
"You're right," he said to my Human, "She is a real live-wire."

"Wow! That wasn't so bad." I meowed as I joined Molly in the cage.

A valuable lesson had been learned that day. Now I understood that the clinic was a safe and loving place. I had learned that my veterinarian Dr.

Piper was my friend. His assistants were kind and caring people who really loved animals. They thought that I was the cat's meow.

My first visit to *The Lakemont Veterinary Clinic* was just the beginning of a beautiful relationship between Dr. Piper and myself.

Chapter 5
The Baby Shower

It wasn't long after Molly's and my arrival that my Human had been invited out to dinner. She had no more than left the house when a stream of ladies came bursting through the backdoor. Chattering voices along with hardy laughter really startled me and the orange and white, with the big fluffy tail and the long white whiskers.

Now because of my young age I didn't know much about human folks yet, but my feline intuitions told me that this group was certainly up to no good. Several of the ladies hurried about hanging balloons and streamers all over the place.

"Oh my goodness," I said to myself, "Mom will think I created this mess."

Molly and I didn't know what to make of the situation or which way to run to get out of the way.

27

Maggie and Molly

In a flash, poor Molly went scurrying under the couch, her almond colored eyes peering out in astonishment. I wasn't far behind her. After a short time Molly nudged me. I knew that she wanted me to investigate.

"Be brave!" I said to myself, as I crept out from under the couch. After all I was the bravest and most curious feline in the house.

Then in my sassiest voice I yelled,

"Enough! Enough already! Who are you and what are you doing in my Human's house? Mom will think that I let in strangers. Meow! Meow!" I continued until one of the intruders, whose hair was the same color as Molly's looked down and asked, "What have we here?"

"I'm a cat," I snarled under my breath, "and there is another one crouched under the couch."

"Oh my, this sassy little rascal has to be Maggie," said the lady. "Come on girls we have to find Molly too. After all these furry little critters are the guests of honor."

Shortly after my confrontation with the lady, who had the orange-blond hair, other human folks had started arriving at the backdoor. Such jibber jabber you never heard. They placed brightly colored bags and packages of all sizes and shapes on the living room floor. I noticed that Molly and my names were written on them. There were even a few packages for Mom too.

A very large cake was put in the center of the dining room table. It actually had two cats and a bunch of flowers painted on it.

"Yummy," I thought.

I would have loved to have crawled up and put my paws in it, but one of the silly ladies stood guard and she would not allow me to go near the table.

Since I was too little to count I wasn't sure how many human folks showed up that night. I do know that they were a fine group of ladies who knew how to throw a party.

I scampered back to the couch. Peeking under I coaxed Molly to come out and take a closer look. Just as the orange and white, with the big fluffy tail and the long white whiskers, got up enough courage to crawl out from under the couch, all the lights went out. The chattering and the laughter came to an abrupt halt and everyone there seemed to hold their breath.

"It's Mom! It's my Human! What will she think of all these intruders?" I wondered to myself.

Just as the front door opened the lights came on again and all the silly ladies yelled, "Surprise!"

"I can't believe it," shrieked my Human.
"As a matter of fact no one would ever believe you have done such a crazy thing." Mom laughed until tears rolled down her cheeks. Many of the gals were busy taking pictures. One lady made a video of the whole evening.

Molly and I stood frozen in our tracks. Our Human picked us up and kissed the top of our furry little heads like she always did. Then she said,

"Girls, this party is for you. It's a Baby Shower to welcome you to my family."

Things seemed much better now that Mom was back. She sat on the living room floor with Molly and me on her lap. All three of us opened packages of wonderful kitty surprises. Molly and I played with the ribbons and bows and the brightly colored paper. We opened gift after gift, all of which delighted my Human. Mom got a pink shirt that read **Owner of the World's Cutest Cats**. She wore it a lot.

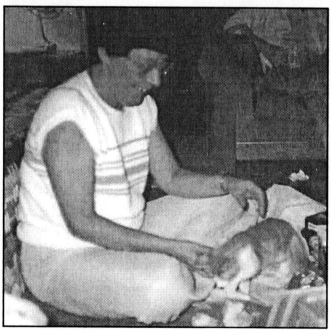

Mom at the Baby Shower

Mom at the Baby Shower

Molly had never been much of a show off, but she was so excited after rolling in the crumpled up gift-wrap that she really let loose that night. She snatched a furry little catnip mouse by the tail and she ran to the kitchen with it dangling from her mouth. Everyone really laughed at her. Out of curiosity I followed my sister to the kitchen to see what she was up to. You'll never believe what she did. She drowned that catnip mouse in our bowl of drinking water. Then she darted back to join the party.

After Molly and I had romped around the room for some time I grew tired and curled up on my Human's lap for a nap. Lying there I wondered if all human folks did such silly things or just Mom's friends. It was surely a night to remember.

Molly and Snowboy

Chapter 6
Snowboy

As I recall the winter sky hung heavy with snow and the strong north wind blew drifts into cotton-like hills throughout the neighborhood. It wasn't a fit day for man or beast. A man who stayed inside a strange box on the kitchen counter told all humans and pets to stay indoors. Tons of snow had been falling and the temperature was well below zero. Major highways had drifted shut and all the local streets and roads were closed except for emergency vehicles. No one was to venture outdoors until the snow emergency was lifted.

Mom looked at Molly and me huddled in front of the hot air vent. She announced that she did not have to go to school because of the blizzard. Now I didn't know exactly what that meant, but I thought it had to do with the white stuff falling from the sky.

My Human put on her long blue chenille robe, poured a cup of steaming coffee and then she began to get our breakfast ready. I loved it when my Human stayed home from school. I called it my pampering day.

After a hearty breakfast and a fresh drink of water, I climbed onto the windowsill to keep a watchful eye on my territory. It was quite difficult to see outside because a heavy accumulation of frost covered the windows.

Now I had a rather keen sense of knowing when something invaded my space. There was something moving slowly through the drifts of snow. It was coming closer and closer to my Human's house.

"Psst! Psst! Molly, come here," I beckoned.
After a yawn and a stretch, the orange and white, with the big bushy tail and the very long whiskers, joined me on the windowsill. Being quite smart, Molly took her warm little paw and she rubbed it in a circular motion against the frosted glass.
"Wow," I stammered, "you made a magic peek hole."
Then Molly motioned for me to do the same.

We sat astounded as a scrawny yellow figure approached the house.
"Yikes," I yelled, "It's a heline!"
We both ran for cover.

Our curiosity soon brought us back to the ledge. The heline was gone. Molly and I sat gibbering about our discovery when Mom arrived to see what we were up to. Then she noticed the tracks in the snow too.

"Oh no," she said. "There's a poor little creature out in this horrible, horrible storm."

Without any hesitation, my Human got dressed in her warmest clothing and headed for the backyard. In no time at all she returned to the warmth of the kitchen. Shivering she said, "Girls, I can't find anything but tracks outside."

Molly and I continued to keep a vigil at the kitchen window for several days. At last the heline reappeared. We chattered excitedly letting our Human know that he was back.

Mom came to the kitchen window and there, outside in the snow sat the little orphan. "It's a c-a-t," she whispered. "I think he is homeless," she continued.

Our Human hurried to my bag of food and she poured a generous amount into a bowl. Then she rushed to the backyard and set the food on an old picnic table. When she returned all three of us watched anxiously as the scrawny little thing gobbled down every last morsel. Then he quickly retreated from the yard.

Early the next morning Mom built a make shift shelter on the old picnic table for the heline. She filled it with dry straw and she placed a little woolen blanket inside it too. Then Mom filled a dish to overflowing with food, which she put into the shelter for the homeless little cat.

Each day the heline, whom I affectionately named Snowboy, spent more and more time in the shelter. He would peek through the kitchen windows to flirt with Molly and me.

In no time at all Snowboy allowed Mom to pet him. He would even roll about in the snow so that Mom would rub his belly. Then one cold and windy morning, as Mom opened the backdoor, Snowboy bolted past her and darted into the warmth of the kitchen. At that moment I knew in my heart that the heline was here to stay.

Mom named him Max.

Now we are four, Molly, Mom, Max and me.

Chapter 7
Shenanigans

By now you must realize that I was quite the mischievous cat. Ordinary had never been part of my kitty vocabulary.

One boring morning, after my Human had left for school, I went roaming around the house in search of Molly and Max. To my amazement Mom had left the door open between the kitchen and the enclosed back porch. It was early spring and there was still a chill in the air. Instead of perching myself at a window to watch the many wonders of the season, I promptly jumped up on the counter and slithered onto the microwave. Then magically my back legs sprang like coils as I hurled myself into the air landing on top of the open door. "Wow! What a feat," I said out loud. "My Human should have seen that one."

Molly and Max appeared out of nowhere. They begged me to come down.

"Meow, meow," they pleaded again and again.

However, I the amazing cat was having too much fun showing off for my friends to get down. Then timid Max accidentally bumped the door and it swung miles away from the microwave and counters. Every time I tried to move, the door moved further away. So there I stayed clinging to the top of the door while Molly and Max sat comfortably on the back porch, watching the wonders of spring and the many little animals searching for food.

"Drats!" I murmured.

The hours passed slowly and my ribs had begun to hurt from lying in such an awkward position all day. Finally I heard the sound of Mom's car. "She's home at last," I whispered to myself. Molly met her at the front door to let her know that I had once again gotten myself into a jam. As my Human walked into the kitchen, she spied me clinging precariously to my perch. I knew that I would soon be her arms. Mom laughed and grabbed the camera. "Get me down," I insisted, "This is not a time for a picture." Then my Human got on a chair and she lifted me off my horrid perch and held me in her arms. I licked her nose in thanks. I was starving, so I wiggled free to eat my breakfast and lunch. After all, if I didn't hurry I'd miss dinner.

Mischief was my middle name. I remember the day I went on a scary jaunt through the ductwork of our home. The old heat registers that were embedded in the floors had always intrigued me. For years I wanted to explore them. Then one day to my surprise a carpenter came to make some changes in the floor registers. Just as he lifted the covering from a large cool air return I scooted past him and down I went. At that very moment Mom screeched, "Maggie, No!" It was too late. I was on a journey to explore the darkened tin tunnel that ran throughout the basement. "What a maze!"

Maggie

I had a wonderful time exploring as I crawled about knocking down cobwebs and collecting dust balls along the way.

My Human's pleas for me to come out echoed throughout the tin tunnel. My newly discovered playground was fascinating. Mom's cries for my return were useless.

"What if she's stuck somewhere," my Human asked? I could hear her worried voice vibrating in the tunnel, but I continued on my merry way.

The workman hurried to the basement. He began banging on the outside of my maze with a metal instrument. It sounded like rolling thunder as I scampered back toward the opening and into the arms of my Human.

There were no hugs and kisses as Mom promptly put me into the spare bedroom and closed the door. She didn't even take my picture and I was a sight to behold. There were cobwebs hanging from my whiskers and layers of dust covered my calico coat.

I spent the rest of the afternoon cleaning myself. "Uck!" Antique cobwebs and ancient dust really didn't taste very good.

The prissy orange and white with the big fluffy tail and the extra long whiskers just sat and shook her head. As for Max, he stretched from a peaceful nap and cuddled close to me. I knew he was wondering why I couldn't stay out of trouble and just how long it would be until my next adventure.

Well, it wasn't long. My impulsive nature got the best of me again. I had never been out-doors in my whole entire life. Since exploring and curiosity were such a big part of my nature I had decided to make a run for it the next chance I got.

While Mom cleaned the kitchen, I laid in wait. I knew that she would be taking the trash to the big gray can in the backyard. As soon as she opened the door I darted between her legs and away I went. The grass carpet beneath my feet tickled. I ran as fast as my little legs would go.

"Oh, no," Mom shouted! "Maggie, stop!" She dropped the garbage and the chase was on. I ran and ran and ran. I was a least a half block away before I even looked back. When I finally looked up I was face to face with two huge dogs. "Opps!" I had invaded their territory.

"Woof, woof, woof," they protested loudly. "Get out of our yard, cat!"

I high-tailed it back home, passing Mom and a neighbor along the way.

"Maggie, stop," Mom insisted, but I kept running. I hid myself under a bush in my neighbor's yard. The sound of my heart beating loudly must have given my hiding place away. My Human reached under the bush. She picked me up and I snuggled close to her heart.

"Your mischievous ways get you into so much trouble," Mom said. She took me back into the safety of my home, gave me time out and I gave her an attitude. Then she returned to the yard to pick up the trash.

"I really love my Human," I said out loud.

Maggie's Attitude

Do you remember the jovial old lady with the twinkle in her bright blue eyes? I think I inherited my mischievous ways from her.

My Grandma liked to play tricks on Mom too. During one of our many visits up the mountain, Grandma had coaxed me into her bedroom by shaking a can of my favorite treats. Then she got into an old brown chest and pulled out a box of treasures that had been Mom's when she was a baby.

"Hush Maggie," she whispered as she slipped me into one of my Human's knit baby outfits. Grandma started to laugh. She was the only human I knew who actually made a deep belly laugh.

"Ha! Ha! Ha!" She laughed out loud.

Mom was in the living-room watching a football game. Just as she got up to see what was going on, Grandma rounded the corner of the living-room with me in her arms. They both laughed until tears rolled down Mom's cheeks. I must admit that I was as cute as could be in the fancy pink baby outfit.

Lois M. Werfel

Grandma and Maggie

Tabby and Tessa

Chapter 8
The Promise

Molly, Max and I had gotten quite used to our regular visits to Grandma's place. She continued to spoil us with hugs, kisses and our favorite treats. Nobody could shake a treat can quite like Grandma.

For weeks Mom had been traveling the mountain without us. She would leave right after work and come home long after the moon came out.

One morning my Human gathered us around her. I could tell she was worried. She said, "Grandma's heart broke and it had to be fixed. We are going to pack our belongings and move up the mountain to care for her during the summer months." That explained why Mom went back and forth without us.

Grandma had two cats of her own. Compared to me, Tessa and Tabby were real pussycats. Mom had gotten them for her about the same time she adopted Molly and me. I think they were a surprise for her eightieth birthday. That would have made them a tad over five years old.

Tessa and Tabby as Kittens

Our summer at Grandma's house was different from our other visits. The jovial old lady with the twinkle in her bright blue eyes had lost her spark. She spent most of each day in bed. Molly, Max, Tessa, Tabby and I took turns lying on her bed to comfort her. Her frail little hands would rub up and down our backs as if to say I love you.

Each day Mom would tell me how very proud she was that I was being such a good girl. I knew that this was not the time for mischief.

One morning during our stay Max came up lame. To this day we don't know how he injured himself. Mom took him to Tessa and Tabby's vet. When she returned Max wasn't with her. My heart broke too. I wondered if Grandma's doctors could fix it. Then I heard Mom tell Grandma that the ligaments in Max's leg were torn and must be fixed. Mom would be able to bring him home the next day. I spread the word among the other cats and we were all quite relieved.

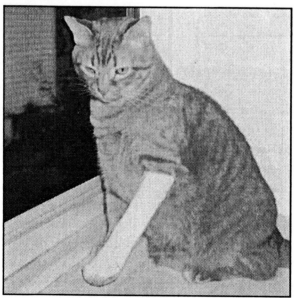

Max with a Cast on His Leg

When Max came home he had a metal splint on his leg with a cast all around it. At first, he hobbled around. In no time at all he was moving quite well, except for the thump, thump, thumping sound he made when he walked across the floor.

It was getting toward the end of summer and Mom had to go home to prepare for the new school term because she was a school teacher.

She told us that our aunt from Minnesota was flying home to watch over Grandma.

"Wow," I said, "She must be something special if she can fly." I could not wait to see this marvel.

Before we left for home, Mom sat on the edge of Grandma's bed and talked quietly with her for a long time. On our way down the mountain Mom announced that she promised to bring Tessa and Tabby to our house to live. Grandma was just too sick to care for them any longer. Trying to make light of the situation my Human said,

"After all guys, cats are like potato chips, you can't have just one."

"Yep," I said, "Mom will give Tessa and Tabby a good home." In unison, Molly and Max agreed that there was none better than ours. Now I didn't exactly like the idea of two more cats moving in until the orange and white with the big fluffy tail and the extra long whiskers reminded me that I had once been an orphan myself.

The next morning Mom left the house carrying the two small blue carriers. She returned that evening with our new feline residents, Tabby and Tessa. They seemed to know that they were here to stay. Now we are six, Molly, Max, Tessa, Tabby, Mom and me.

Tabby

Tessa

In a few short days the jovial old lady with the twinkle in her bright blue eyes had passed away.

It was a difficult time for all of us, especially my Human.

Chapter 9
Along Came Kitty

In the summer of 1996, another "potato chip" arrived. I guess Mom just couldn't control herself. If there had been a Cat's Anonymous, all the felines and the one heline in this house would certainly sign her up.

Miss Kitty

I was napping at the front window when a middle-aged man appeared at the door. "Here she is," the man announced. One whiff and I knew it was that cat mom had been hanging around with at work. I had smelled that scent hundreds of times. Believe me, the nose knows.

The other cats encircled the cage. They all took a whiff and in turn walked slowly away. Not me! I sat boldly and stared at the cat, then at the man. A loud hiss exploded from my mouth. My Human was quite embarrassed that I'd do such a thing to our guest.

"I know their game," I thought to myself. They wanted me to believe that Mom was going to be a cat nanny for only a few days and that the man would come back for the brat in the cage.

The man talked politely for a few minutes and then he left. "Five's enough!" I shouted as soon as Mom closed the door. But she promptly took the caged cat into the spare bedroom and shut the door behind her.

"No, oh no," I shrieked, "She's done it again." This was my Human's way of breaking in a new arrival. That cat was here to stay. I wish Mom didn't like potato chips so much!

Mom went in and out of the spare room at least a dozen times that night, as I sat pouting outside the door.

"Good girl, Maggie," she would say each time.

"Yeah, right!" was my sarcastic remark.

My vivid imagination ran wild. I just knew that Mom was on the bed petting that furry little creature. She was probably brushing her fur and trimming her claws.

"Pamper, pamper, pamper," I yelled. Before you know it that cat will be wearing my pink baby outfit and ruling the roost.

It was nearly two weeks before my Human formally introduced us to Kitty. Mom only opened the door to the spare room when she was home. Kitty was a shy scaredy-cat that hid under the bed a lot. She was a small cat with rather short legs and a short tail. She had a very squeaky meow.

Eventually Miss Kitty, as Mom affectionately named her, had begun to come around. The rest of us referred to her as the old lady because she was several years older than any other feline here.

Miss Kitty, Max and I became the best of friends. The others didn't seem to care one way or the other about Kitty's presence. At night Mom's bed was quite a sight. The three of us snuggled as close to her as we could get. Of course, I nestled right under Mom's chin. No cat was going to take my spot. Max slept next to me while the old lady claimed the top of Mom's pillow. Tessa and Tabby had their special places too. Tessa curled behind Mom's right leg and Tabby sprawled close to her stomach. As for Molly, she loved all of us but preferred the comfort of her basket, which rested on top of the nightstand next to the bed. Once in awhile Molly would cuddle with Mom when no other cats were around.

I guess it really didn't matter how many cats Mom had because her love for me got stronger each and every day.

Chapter 10
Cat with a Mohawk

Almost a year after Miss Kitty moved in, I had begun to feel somewhat strange. I was having a problem whenever I tried to use the litter box. Since we were a multi-cat household there were at least five boxes around, but none of which seemed to work for me.

Mom noticed that I had begun to throw-up a little here and there. The natural assumption was that I had a dreaded fur ball, so she gave me a couple of doses of fur ball treatment. But that didn't help me at all.

One day, while Mom was at school, I got really sick, sicker than I had ever been before. I crawled into a corner, curled up and there I stayed too weak to move. "No mischief today," I thought. Molly, Max, Tessa, Tabby and Miss Kitty checked on me throughout the day but there was nothing they could do.

"My Human will make me better when she gets home," I whispered faintly. Then I dozed off for a long nap.

Molly and Maggie

When Mom entered the house I heard her say to Molly, "That's strange, Maggie isn't at her usual post at the front window. She always runs to greet me with her tail raised high and tipped a little at the end."

"Maggie, Maggie, where are you," she called?

I was just too sick to answer. She began a room-by-room search until she finally found me huddled in the corner of her bedroom next to the dresser.

"What's wrong, Love Bug?" she asked.

I meowed in the softest of cries as she lifted me onto the bed. When I didn't respond to her tender touches she knew that there was something drastically wrong with me. She reached for the apparatus and called Dr. Piper's office. I didn't even protest when Mom wrapped me in a blanket and slipped me into the cage.

In a flash, we arrived at the Lakemont Veterinary Clinic. Miss Receptionist told Mom that Dr. Piper wasn't in.

"Another doctor will see Maggie today," she said.

"Oh no," I whimpered. "This is an emergency and I want my own doctor."

Mom had to stay in the waiting room while a technician drew some blood. I was frightened but still I acted bravely. After a brief time I was returned to the examining room and my Human was ushered in.

"I'm afraid Maggie has a kidney problem," said the new doctor. "She is also dehydrated and needs to be put on I.V. fluids. Maggie will have to be admitted."

Mom signed a paper so that I could stay. The staff had Mom's permission to do X-rays and more blood tests in the morning. Mom's eyes filled with tears at the thought of my being sick. She was heart-sick that she had to leave me alone at the clinic, even though it was for the best.

Mom returned the next afternoon to meet with the doctor. He put up some strange looking pictures that actually showed my insides, bones, organs and all. Of all the pictures I've ever seen of me I thought these had to be the silliest, but my Human didn't laugh. It seemed that both my kidneys had crystals and my condition was not reversible. A change in my diet and a daily dose of I.V. fluids might slow the disease but would not cure me. Before we left the clinic one of the technicians taught Mom how to give me fluids.

At home all my furry friends gathered around to greet me.

"Yea! Maggie's home," they yelled! "Boy, did we miss you."

Max bumped my nose and licked my face all over. What a kiss! Even though Max and I were complete opposites we were the perfect couple. The prissy orange and white with the big fluffy tail and the extra long whiskers snuggled next to me and whispered, "I love you, Maggie."

Even thought I didn't always cooperate, Mom changed my food and she gave me a daily dose of fluids. I felt bad for her. At first she would actually break out in a cold sweat when she inserted the needle. She had placed the I.V. bag on a hook on which was on the front of the bedroom door. It reminded me of the clinic.

Eventually though, she could give my fluids in a slick fashion. I had become accustomed to our daily ritual and waited quietly on the bed. I guess this is what spending quality time with your loved ones means.

For a time I felt like my old self. Then I began feeling sick again. Mom recognized the signs now. We headed for the clinic.

"Dr. Piper will see Maggie now," said Miss Receptionist. My heart danced with joy.
"He's here," I said softly. "Let's go, I want to see my friend."

My blood work showed that once again I was in trouble. My kidneys had not been filtering the poisons from my system. I was admitted to the clinic for about three suns. I didn't really mind because everyone there pampered me to no end. Mom visited me each day. She really missed me. After all I was her first kitty and her number one squeeze.

Before my release Dr. Piper talked seriously about my medical condition. Since I was such a special cat the decision was made to operate and clean the crystals from my kidneys. I went home for a few days to visit with my family and to get some tender loving care from my Human.

I thought it was strange that Mom fed me only once the day before my first surgery.

"I want food!" I demanded. "I'm half starved and thirsty too."

"Maggie, I'm only following doctor's orders," said Mom.

When the new sun came up, Mom put me in my cage. Molly, Max, Tessa, Tabby and Miss Kitty crowded around to say goodbye. Then they scurried off for a hearty breakfast.

"What friends!"

My surgery went well. That afternoon Mom returned to the clinic to talk with Dr. Piper.

"The kidney we operated on today was somewhat deformed," he told my Human.

"Maggie isn't out of the woods yet. That kidney will have to do the job when we operate on the other side," he said.

"Maggie's spunk and determination will get her through this," Mom said. "This little cat wants to live."

I was at the clinic for many suns and moons. At first I was woozy and somewhat uncomfortable. Mom's daily visits along with her hugs and kisses were my best medicine. Dr Piper and his entire staff were wonderful. After a while I felt as thought I was on vacation at one of those fancy animal spas.

I couldn't wait to go home and crawl onto my Human's lap. Then one day Dr. Piper said, "Maggie's doing fine, except she is not eating.

Let's send her home today. This might stimulate her appetite."

I did eat better in my own surroundings. My recovery went well. Many of Mom's friends sent me cards and came to see me. They were amazed to learn that my skin pigment was calico in color too. They would laugh and say, "Maggie, you are so cute."

I agreed.

Maggie

The suns and moons passed by quickly. The day came for my second surgery. Once again my family gathered around to wish me well. I wasn't looking forward to the operation, but I did love being cuddled and pampered by Dr. Piper and his staff.

Once again Mom signed the consent forms. Then the left side of my body was shaved for the surgery. There was only a narrow strip of fur left which ran along my backbone. I really did look like a cat with a Mohawk.

The staff reassured me that I would be fine. After all, I was a wonderful patient. Then I went to sleep.

When I awoke I was hooked up to an IV and other medications to help fight infection.
"Meow," I said softly. "I don't feel so good," I murmured.

"Come on Maggie," said one of the girls, "you are such a brave little cat. Use some of that spunkiness and you'll pull through this rough time."
"I'm trying," I whispered softly.
Knowing that Mom called several times that day helped.

The next morning Mom received a call at work informing her that my condition had worsened. They put me on a heating pad to warm my body temperature. But I was very weak and in need of a blood transfusion. One of the technicians, who worked with Dr. Piper, brought her cat, Miss Rouser, to the clinic so that I could be transfused.

By the next morning I had begun to feel better. Miss Rouser probably saved my life. She is a real cataterian and my hero. Mom sent her a cat toy and a trophy filled with kitty treats.

Miss Rouser

After a few days Mom was allowed to visit me at the clinic. She did so for many suns to come. Then the big day arrived for returning home. Naturally, I was more spoiled than before.

Chapter 11
The Last Dance

At last there was quality back in my life. Now I needed two daily does of fluids to help keep my kidneys flushed out. Other than that life seemed rather normal.

Maggie

My very favorite thing to do with my Human was to dance to Willie Nelson's song, "*Blue Eyes Crying In the Rain.*" I honestly don't know why I chose this particular song, but I did. Mom could play any tape, but when the first beat of Willie's song played I was there, begging to be picked up. Everybody would laugh out loud as I nestled around Mom's neck to dance and kiss her cheek. Mom made it a point to dance with me everyday before she left for work.

The months passed as I played and frolicked with my furry companions. Molly and Max were especially happy to see me back in true form. Mom was quite happy because she had her lap cat back.

During the summer of 1999 I again began experiencing some of the symptoms of kidney failure again. I didn't tell my Human right away because she was so happy. It wasn't long until Mom picked up on what was happening to me. Her heart sank to the bottom of her tummy.

My appetite was gone and the old litter box problem had started again. Even thought Mom hated to do it, she took me back to the clinic.

After several days Dr Piper said, "Take Maggie home and keep her comfortable."

At home Mom tried everything imaginable to get me to eat.

"Please, Maggie, you must eat," Mom pleaded.

I couldn't, I just couldn't eat a thing. Mom even liquefied my food and tried feeding me with a syringe. Nothing worked. I simply could not eat.

My strength and my spirit were slipping away. It was even difficult for me to stand now. Mom looked at me with tears in her eyes and she said, "Love Bug, I finally realize now, that I am doing this for me. It's time."

Mom cradled me in her arms and held me close to her heart as we danced to Willie's song. Then a friend drove us to the clinic.

Upon entering the outer office Mom could hardly talk.

"It's time." she said in a whisper.
Miss Receptionist quietly led us to the examining room.

Dr Piper agreed.

"I love you, Maggie." Mom sobbed.
"I love you too Mom." I said with my eyes.

Dr Piper gently gave me two shots.

"Wow, what a trip!"

The next thing I knew I was in the loving arms of the jovial old lady with a twinkle in her bright blue eyes.

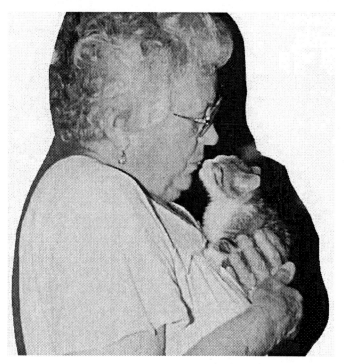

Grandma and Maggie

About the Author

Lois M. Werfel spent most of her life in education as an elementary school teacher and Principal at a Parochial school.

After 44 years of teaching, and sharing her love of cats with her students, Lois retired and now lives in Altoona, PA.

Printed in the United States
39205LVS00001B/1-375

9 781594 083525